Feng Shui

Mastering the Basics to an Elegant Home Design For Inner Peace

By Antonio Barros

Copyright © 2016 by BPI Publishing

All rights reserved

This document attempts to provide exact and reliable information regarding the topics and issues covered. If advice is necessary, legal or professional, a practiced individual should be ordered.

No part of this book may be reproduced in any form or by any electronic or mechanical means, including information storage and retrieval systems, without explicit permission in writing from the publisher or writer, except by a reviewer who may quote brief passages in a published review.

The information provided herein is stated to be truthful and consistent, in that any liability, in terms of inattention or otherwise, by any usage or abuse of any policies, processes, or directions contained within is the solitary and utter responsibility of the recipient reader. Under no circumstances will any legal responsibilities or blame be held against the publisher or writer for any reparation, damages, or monetary loss due to the information herein, either directly or indirectly.

This books makes no guarantees of success or implied promises. Any type of strategy detailed in these pages can work or has worked for others, but results will vary based on individual efforts and circumstances.

1st Edition, June 2016

"Love your home,

And it will love you back.

This is good Feng Shui."

- Rodika Tchi

Table of Contents

Introduction — 7

The Basics of Feng Shui — 9
How Can Feng Shui Help You? — 10
What Feng Shui Is Not: Myths & Misconceptions — 14

A Zen Lifestyle: Essential Principles — 19
Principle 1: Chi in Feng Shui — 20
Principle 2: Connect With Nature — 23
Principle 3: Finding a Balance — 27
Principle 4: Using the Bagua Map — 30
Principle 5: Connectivity & Continuity — 34

Understanding Feng Shui Living — 37
Expression Through Colors — 37

Fitting in Shapes ... 41

Transforming Your Home ... 43

Quick Guide by Directions ... 44

Living Room ... 49

Kitchen ... 52

Bathroom ... 56

Bedroom ... 59

Children's Room ... 63

Office ... 66

Garden ... 69

Declutter & Simplify ... 72

Strategy to Declutter ... 72

Positive Energy Essentials ... 77

Becoming Zen: Perfect Feng Shui Home Tips ... 78

Tip #1 Aromatherapy Always ... 79

Tip #2 Keep Garbage Covered ... 80

Tip #3 Quality Air & Light Matters	80
Tip #4 Plants in Every Room	81
Tip #5 Don't Overdo It	82
Get Started Today	83

Parting Words   **84**

Introduction

To be able to master Feng Shui, you first need to know what it is. Essentially, Feng Shui is a system of arranging your home or general surroundings to promote harmony and balance with the natural world that surrounds you. The words Feng Shui translate into 'wind and water' in Chinese. The elements and energy certainly do play a significant role within mastery of this spiritual concept. Feng Shui, however, is a practical and contemporary approach to use what you have to bring good things into your life. It is about finding balance within your home, and thereby within yourself.

There are different principles related to the art of Feng Shui, which this book will take you through step by step. To help make sure that you can bring balance and harmony into your home with what you already have, only your personal effort is required. It is not needed to spend a lot of money on your home arrangements to make sure that you are bringing good fortune into your life. This book will take you through all the essentials that you need to know to get started and improve your home with the guidelines of the famous Feng Shui concepts.

Remember that Feng Shui doesn't have to be a drastic change – simply incorporating Feng Shui principles on a long term basis will help to get you going with implementing a newly found balance into your life. Never hurry things, but take your time to think about the best solutions, this is what the Eastern religious masters have taught me for years. The Western culture is often times too obsessed with drastic changes, while this might impact their life balance significantly and drastically. However, I'd like you to take a different approach. Do what you can, as you can, and this mastery guide to the art of Feng Shui will help you to have a home that brings good fortune, prosperity and balance for a long time to come.

The Basics of Feng Shui

Feng Shui, in its essence, is the practice of bringing harmony and balance into your surroundings, so that you can connect with the natural world and your inner energy. In it's core, it is nothing more than 'The Art of Placement': it allows you to know what to put where, which shapes, colors and materials to use, as well as to create a home environment focused on personal happiness and balance.

Incorporating principles of Feng Shui into your life is said to bring you good fortune. The principles stem from an ancient Eastern spiritual tradition. Feng Shui has a rich history, and it spans over thousands of years. It is said that incorporating the principles will help a person to enforce a gradual shift within their personal lives by making subtle changes within the personal space. This is done to access the deeper consciousness and influence the personal self-image and energy balance.

How Can Feng Shui Help You?

Harmonizing yourself with your environment, which is the goal of Feng Shui, has many proven benefits that have been seen time and time again. You will *feel* more of the benefits of Feng Shui than see them, such as feeling good vibrations from a living space that is in harmony.

These good vibrations will help people to feel more comfortable and more productive in the work as well as the home environment. You'll find many of the benefits of Feng Shui listed below.

- **Mindfulness:** You'll become more mindful of the small things when you are practicing and actively incorporating Feng Shui into your living or working space. This can be a good thing, as many people focus too much on the big picture and they'll miss important minor details that make the big picture possible. If you allow 'minor' problems or influencers of imbalances to pile up, then you are more likely to accumulate stress. With Feng Shui, you learn to take care of even the minor problems, allowing you to become more productive. It can even help you to put off procrastination for the same reason.

- **Fresh Perspective:** Feng Shui can give you a fresh perspective, which is always welcome. It can invite change in your life for the better, and when you can look at your living space in a new light, then you can feel refreshed. Your perspective is no longer being dragged down by the negative that was existing in the space, and you are able to concentrate on the future.

- **Balance without Clutter:** Everyone needs balance in their life, but so few people will actually achieve balance. With clutter burdening you, you will find yourself unnecessarily stressed out. When introducing Feng Shui, you are introducing balance into your life through the removal of any type of clutter in your living space. You are incorporating elements into your space that give you a sense of control while connecting you to the natural world, making you feel more at peace with where you are.

- **Inviting Success:** Feng Shui invites success and prosperity into your life because it has a positive disposition. It will invite positive energy vibrations into your life, as stated before, but this will also attract good people and opportunities that you may not have had before, simply because other people will sense that you are more balanced yourself. This balance will attract others towards you and make them more likely to aid you in any way possible. You might also become more confident and happier in your work environment, which in turn could lead to career success as well.

- **Aesthetic Appeal:** Feng Shui living spaces look beautiful when done properly, and the peaceful design brings a well-decorated look to your home or office. The techniques have been honed through generation after generation, bringing beauty in both aspect and design into your space.

- **Meet New People:** When you are learning about Feng Shui, you can find like-minded people and meet new people that are happy to bring balance into your life. It doesn't matter how much knowledge you have already. There is always something to learn, and many Feng Shui enthusiast are a tight community, very helpful and they are likely to give you new tips and tricks that will enhance your spiritual learning.

What Feng Shui Is Not: Myths & Misconceptions

You now know what Feng Shui is, but it's important that you know what Feng Shui *is not* as well. There are many myths and misconceptions surrounding the practice that may turn you away or mislead from this beneficial practice. This section dispels these myths and misconceptions, so that you can start your Feng Shui journey today. Some of these myths might seem unclear or out of context for people that have just started learning about Feng Shui, but as you read further into the book you will understand the concepts behind some of these myths much better. It is important to debunk some persistent myths early on, however, so it is good to know that some ideas surrounding Feng Shui are not necessarily true or accurate. Let's take a look at some persistent myths.

- **Myth #1 The Red Door:** A red colored door can be seen as bringing luck in Feng Shui, but it is not suited for every house. It is a successful use of the color, but it will depend on different factors on if it is best for the front door for you. You have to look at the way the door is facing and then you can choose the best color for your house. You don't have to worry about painting your door red if you don't want to. Be open to different possibilities.

- **Myth #2 No Flowers in the Bedroom:** A lot of people think that fresh flowers can't be put in the bedroom if you are practicing Feng Shui. Once again, you have to be specific. Not every flower is going to be bad in your bedroom. Fresh flowers have good energy or 'chi' as it's called. It can bring sweet healing scents into your home as well as a sense of enchantment. There is no issue in putting flowers in most rooms, as they can really help you with the connection to nature that is so important within the Feng Shui principles.

- **Myth #3 Instant Change with Furniture:** So many people seem to think that Feng Shui is as simple as moving your furniture. They even go as far as to believe that moving your furniture is going to bring instant change and success within your life. That may be a nice fantasy, but it is simply just that, a fantasy. You can't do something that simple and expect such immediate, grand results. Feng Shui is not a miracle cure that will fall from the sky, it is a process of cange that will happen over time. When you change your furniture around often, you are promoting an energy flow in your house. Fresh energy is going to have an effect on your life, especially an effect on your psychologically. This could lead to change, but it will not produce an immediate, grand change like a promotion.

- **Myth #4 Luck & Money with the Right Plant:** Again, there is nothing so small that you can change to have a large and immediate effect. The right plant can help, but it will not solve all of your issues. There are several plants to bring monetary gain in Feng Shui, and you will want to explore the options to see which is best for you. Of course, any plant that is lush, healthy, and vibrant can bring abundance into your life through time because it has a soft, flowing energy. It replicates nature, and so it's important to take care of the plants you have and get one that fits your space.

- **Myth #5 Your Bed Must Face a Certain Way:** You are not doomed if your bed isn't facing a lucky direction. Don't worry about it that much. If you can get it to face a lucky direction, then good for you, but it is not necessary. It will certainly not bring you misfortune if it is facing in the wrong direction. The way you get up in the morning may be important, but not on such a grand scale. After all, it is more about how your personal living space makes you feel rather than the exact positioning – Feng Shui implemented with some minor deviation from the principles will not cancel out the positive effects automatically.

- **Myth #6 Love & Mandarin Ducks:**
Mandarin ducks will not bring everlasting love. They are the most popular as well as classical Feng Shui cure for love, but it doesn't promise a devoted, loyal spouse. It just promotes a lasting happiness, but it's not a miracle. Just see them as a symbol for love and good fortune, but in the end acting from love is all up to yourself and will not be magically implemented from an object into your personal life.

- **Myth #7 Bagua Mirrors Protecting Your Home:** The first thing you need to know about a bagua mirror is that they should never be inside of your home no matter if they are concave or not. They are meant to be outside, and only if you have energy attacking your home. This energy can also be called *Sha Chi*. They're not even needed to protect your house from negative energy directed at it. We will learn all about what a bagua exactly is later on.

A Zen Lifestyle: Essential Principles

In this chapter you'll find the five basic power principles of Feng Shui. These make up the core of the art of understanding and implementing Feng Shui successfully. You should get a grasp on these conceptis if you aim to implement and master Feng Shui concepts in your home. From learning to adjust your *chi* to knowing how everything should be connected, Feng Shui becomes easier.

When you understand the principles that make up every rule you need to follow, you are on your path towards a more balanced lifestyle. This will bring peace, calmness and harmony in your life, but only when applied properly and consistently.

Principle 1: Chi in Feng Shui

Chi is an energy force which is constantly moving and changing. It is what makes you feel good or bad in different locations, and the point of Feng Shui is to adjust chi energy, so that you have balance. You don't want chi to rapidly leave your space, and it's important that you keep the chi in your area flowing gently throughout your indoor environment. Essentially, it is nothing more than vital energy that comes from objects, nature, people, and your environment as a whole.

Chi is a living energy, and it is always swirling and in motion. In nature, chi flows and movies like the water or wind. However, when you build a living environment, you often are surrounded by too many sharp angles or straight lines. These shapes and edges will keep chi from moving properly in your office or home, and should therefore be avoided as much as possible. You don't want to break the positive flow of chi, and so you need to adjust your living space or works pace accordingly. Chi can either manifest itself to be negative or positive, and therefore you will sometimes need to bring about a change in chi until it feels just right to you. This exactly is the energy balance we are trying to achieve through the art of Feng Shui.

If you are trying to understand positive chi, then just picture a comfortable place for you. Think of a place that makes you feel at home, and then try to picture the colors, decorations, aromas, fabrics, and try to pin point what made you feel happy and welcome. You'll notice it was the little things that promoted good energy within the area. This is what is referred to as being positive chi. This is what we are after, but we don't want to have too much of it as we are seeking a balance. Negative chi is always present, so a balance is usually found in introducing positive chi in a space of negative chi. An example of negative chi would be a space or location where you felt uncomfortable. Concentrate on all of those details that make you feel that way and attempt to make a list for yourself what those negative elements are. For example, an office may have been too harsh with white walls or the metal desks could have seemed to sharp. You may have even though that the lighting was too harsh or the smell is strange. It could even be the material of the objects surrounding you, or the airflow. A lot of different factors can create negative chi, and the difficulty lies in finding these exact factors and changing them towards positivity.

Chi can also become blocked or stuck, which can have a negative effect on your everyday life and general surroundings. This is called a *sha chi*. It can affect your spiritually, emotionally and even physically when your home or office is filled with sha chi. Negative chi or sha chi can be seen through things you don't like, things that are cluttered, or even things that are broken. You should attempt to live by the three R's, which are Replace, Repair and Remove. Replace objects that have sha chi. Repair the damage done by the blocked energy through incorporating new objects. Remove sharp edges or straight lines in home design to keep negative chi away from your space.

Principle 2: Connect With Nature

When using Feng Shui, it is important that you include natural elements in your home, and the easiest way to do this is to use the colors of each of the elements, tying them into your home decor. Below you'll find the five essential elements to use, and what they mean in terms of Feng Shui living.

- **Wood:** Wood is possible the most essential of the five elements of Feng Shui, as it is an element often found in nature. You will find that it enhances self-awareness, intuition, creativity, personal growth and flexibility. Green and purple will add the element of wood into your home, and you can make additions of objects made of wood, including blinds, patterns that represent the trunk of a tree, live plants, artwork illustrating landscapes or plants, vertical wooden objects or even furniture.

- **Fire:** Fire is another key element of Feng Shui, and it is best when you need to use it for renewal, excitement, and even transformation. You should never place your fire elements directly next to your water elements (another important element category), since they are opposing forces. When wanting to add the element of fire into your home, you can use the colors yellow, orange and red. Stoves, fireplaces, candles, and all forms of lighting can represent fire. Artwork that depicts pets, wildlife, bright flowers or sunshine can also bring fire into your room, and you can even use floral arrangements to add the right energy. Diamonds, pyramids, and triangles also represent fire and can help introducing this element as well.

- **Earth:** This element is important when you're trying to get grounding energy in your home. It helps to relieve stress, embed your room with a sense of protection, and even help with focus. You can use the colors olive, beige, light yellow, tan or brown to bring earth energy into your home. They will provide a calming influence to the room. You will need to avoid bright colors, and furnishings such as those that sit lower to the ground or are heavy will work as well. Soft cushions, wooden pedestals, built in bookshelves, natural stone, square and rectangular shapes embedded in pottery, and exposed brickwork can bring earth energy as well.

- **Metal:** This element is important when you are trying to focus. It can help increase brainpower and mental intelligence as well. It can also enhance the energies of the rooms themselves, bringing them together like a bridge brings together two parts of land. You can choose gray, white, or any shade of metallic colors to bring the energy of metal into your room. Choose objects that are made of shiny earth metals, coffee tables, end tables, or even chairs with metal legs. Metal planters will usually work best, but you can also use crystal sand gemstones.

- **Water:** This energy will heal and cleanse your mind, spirit and body. It will help you with anything that is holding you back, and it'll bring you a sense of peace and renewal. It will bring insight, clear thinking, a feeling of serenity and peace and even motivation into your life. It can represent both yin and yang. Yang is represented by flowing water, and yin is represented by still water. You can bring aquariums, fish bowls, water features, fountains, reflecting surfaces such as mirrors and glass into your home to bring the energy of water. Artwork depicting water scenes can work as well. Dark blues, black, and various grays can represent water as well.

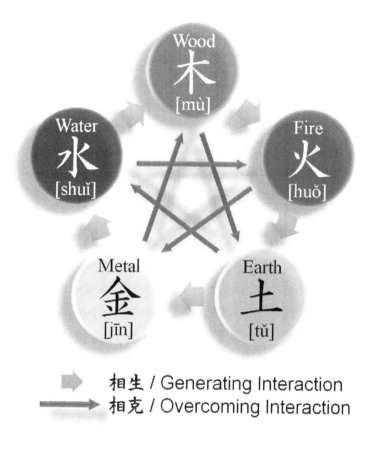

相生 / Generating Interaction
相克 / Overcoming Interaction

Principle 3: Finding a Balance

It is important to find balance in your life, and that requires your yin and yang to be balanced in Feng Shui. You are supposed to achieve balance with the characteristics that are opposing and surround you. These opposing energies are called yin and yang, and with the yin and yang theory which Feng Shui is based around, it states that the universe consists of these opposing forces.

Yin is a feminine force and yang is considered to be a masculine force. The yin qualities are feminine, passive, dark, and nurturing. The yang qualities are seen as being hard, active, aggressive and bright. You find soft and hard, dark and light, and hot and cold all around you.

Yin and yang are natural forces as well, and you need to bring them into balance to find peace and harmony. Most people will balance yin and yang in their home on instinct. You'll add a soft cushion to a hard chair. If water is too hot, you turn on cold water to help. If a wall is too bright, you give it a dark trim. It's instinctual to keep the two in balance, and that's because balance will make you feel at peace, secure, and in general you'll feel more comfortable. When you have an office space that doesn't feel right or a room in general that feels off, it is more than likely that your yin and yang are out of balance.

You will need to add attributes of the missing element to keep balance. If you need more yin, add curves and flowing shapes, dark colors, furniture that is upholstered, place shades on the windows, put rugs on your floor, and add more furniture. If it needs more yang, you'll want angular and straight lines, more light and brighter colors, furniture that is made of stone, glass or wood, bright lights, wood blinds, floors that are made of tile, marble or wood, or even take out some furniture.

Principle 4: Using the Bagua Map

The Bagua Map is a basic tool of Feng Shui, and it's a chart that is used to determine which parts of your home will relate to a specific aspect of your life. For example, some of these aspects can be love, health, or even wealth. It will help you decide where you should place art, objects, and even furniture. If you are able understand the bagua, you'll be able to understand and make adjustments to your living environment according to what the map teaches you.

The traditional bagua is an octagon which contains eight areas (*guas*), and it contains a grounding center, making nine areas that corresponds to critical aspects of your life. It is a grid shape that will contain eight life areas and the grounding center.

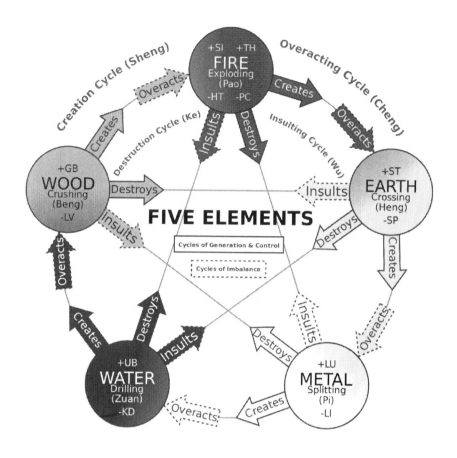

Below, you find the steps needed to use a bagua map.

Step One: You will want to orient the bagua by standing outside of your home at the front door. Look into your home, and as you enter your home through the garage or side door or side door, you'll need to orient it from the true front door of your home.

Step Two: Draw out your floor plan of the first floor of your home, and you'll need to include any attached structures including garages, decks, or side porches. You will need to draw the floor plan for each level of your home. Do not forget to include the basement or attic.

Step Three: You'll then divide it into nine equal areas. Afterwards, you'll need to determine where each room lies within the bagua. When you know what each area represents, you can then add in furniture, colors, and accessories to activate the area. You will be able to tune it to the specific energy that should be in each area.

- **Abundance:** You'll add possessions, collections, fine art, and pictures of any desired objects.
- **Fame/Reputation:** You'll add awards, prizes, diplomas, pictures that represent your future goals, or an image of a sunrise.

- **Love/Relationships:** You'll add photos of you with your significant other, pairs of objects, or pictures of romantic places.
- **Travel/Compassion:** You'll add images that represent your heroes or mentors, successful business projects, or something that represents places you'd like to visit.
- **Career, Work/Self:** You'll add fish tanks, fountains, and artwork depicting moving bodies of water, or items that represent career success in your field.
- **Wisdom/Harmony:** You'll add DVDs, CDs, books, school materials, or any image that makes you feel peaceful.
- **Family/Health:** You'll add photos of friends and family, antiques or heirlooms, or any item that is associated with good health.
- **Balance/Well-Being:** You'll add artwork that depicts mountain landscapes, objects that make you feel secure or grounded, or items that are made of clay or ceramic.

Never overdue adding these objects that depict the area of the bagua you are trying to activate. If you over adjust then you can create an unbalance in your home. A few objects is usually enough. One or two will do the job nicely.

Principle 5: Connectivity & Continuity

This the modern name of the relationship of Feng Shui to Tao. This translates to the path or the way, and it means that every action you take has a reaction. This is a relationship that proves that you are influenced by everything that is around you, and therefore you have an influence on everything as well. This means that decorating your surroundings will influence your life and what you attract in your life. The more you surround yourself with the symbols of what you want, it becomes more likely that you will achieve these goals.

The more these symbols relate to the natural world, the more connected to the natural world that you will feel. You are going to reflect what you are constantly seeing around you. If you are surrounding yourself with express isolation, blackness, or darkness, then you will experience and feel those things. You will end up feeling isolated and lonely. When your furniture is worn down or shabby, then you will feel as if you are stressed out or impoverished. If you continue to let your faucets drip or your toilets continue to run, it is more likely that your wealth will drain away.

Therefore, if you surround yourself with joy, happy images and images of prosperity, then you're more likely to experience joy and prosperity. If your furniture is comfortable, clean, and up to date, you will feel more abundant in your life. If your plumbing works well, then your wealth is not going to dry up. It important you reinforce connectedness. Add symbols of the natural world into your interior rooms, such as rocks, water, plants, and flowers, artworks of nature scenes, aromas, colors, textures, and even natural sounds. By bringing the natural world indoors, you are uplifting the vibrations in your home, bringing peace and harmony to your life. It will bring a sense of calmness and happiness into your life.

Images for Goals:

- **For Career Success:** If you want to power up your career, then you'll want to add images of water. This will help you to attract more wealth. Add it into your work or career area.
- **To Enhance Friendships:** You'll want to add images of people being happy, family or community events, or just pictures of joyous occasions. This will be added in the family area.
- **To Promote Travel:** If you want to promote travel, you'll need to hang scenes of other places in your home. Add gloves or maps, and this will be added in your compassion area.
- **To Enhance or Attract Love:** You'll want to hang images of pairs or objects, including mating birds, and put it in your love or romance area. You can even place pictures of happy couples.

Understanding Feng Shui Living

You already know how to use a bagua map, but there is still more about Feng Shui living that you can learn. You need to be able to understand how to use colors to express what you need to in order to keep chi moving peacefully through your indoor space. Never allow sha chi or negative chi to hang around. Remembering your three R's are only the tip of the iceberg.

Expression Through Colors

Choosing the right colors in your indoor space is incredibly important and will have a major impact on the Feng Shui of your space. With the wrong color choice, negative chi will remain and hang around. The first thing you need to do, is ask yourself who uses the room the most. For example, if it is your child's room, then you'll need colors that work best with your child. These may not be the same colors that work best for you, and you have to keep that in mind. For example, if it's a nursery, you aren't going to want to put red walls in it. It's not going to help the child sleep. Always adjust colors to the purpose of the rooms. We will go into the details for each room in the house later on in this book.

Lively spaces are great with fire colors, and they will help to promote a lively, happy, and energetic space. You can try red, orange, or yellow. These are strong colors, and so you may not want to paint the entire room these colors, but adding them can give a dynamic energy that has people circulating through them. If you want a quieter room, then you'll want to put calming hues such as greens, blues or neutrals.

Don't use just black or white either. You need to strike balance, and using white isn't a neutral when it comes to Feng Shui. White is considered to be a sharp color, as it is fresh and crisp looking. If you are going to use white, give it a darker or off white look. You may even want to use gray. A soft gray is often the right kind of white for proper energy. You shouldn't worry if you just have neutral colors either. Be careful with color pairing as well. You don't want to do a blue and green pairing only for example because it is just for the element of water. You will want to add more than one element to a room so that the energy of that element doesn't overwhelm you. Below you'll find a cheat sheet on how general colors will usually make you feel.

Red: This acts as an active color, so it is a stimulator.

Orange: This is considered to be an uplifting color that will promote happiness in your environment.

Gold/Yellow: This is a color that symbolizes power, stimulates your health, and it can help with both wisdom as well as patience.

Green: Green is a color that represents growth as well as new beginnings. It can also be used for freshness or healing.

Blue-Greens: This will represent youth, a new beginning, and it can inspire a confident energy in your environment.

Deeper Blues: This will help with introspection and infuse wisdom.

Purple: This color inspires you to be more adventurous and spiritual, and it can help it bring prosperity.

Black: Black is a color of contemplation, and it holds mystery. It can also encourage you to reflect on your life.

White: White is a color for clarity, communication and precision.

Grey: This will invite helpfulness in your life. It is also a harmony color because it is a union of white and black.

Brown: This offers security and stability in your life.

Pink: This color represents partnership, romance, and in general it represents feelings of love.

Fitting in Shapes

Each shape in Feng Shui belongs to a specific element. You'll place them in your space to bring energy from this element. Understanding the connection between the preferred shapes and elements is quite simple and straight forwards. We will briefly go over them.

For fire, you'll find that triangles and pyramids will usually work best. Stars will represent the element of fire as well. Square will belong to the element of earth, and it will help you to feel balanced and protected. It will even help you to feel safe and stable. Circular or round shapes belong to the element of metal, and they will bring freshness and clarity. Wavy or flowing shapes will easily represent water in your home.

 Fire - The Tetrahedron

 Water - The Icosahedron

 Air - The Octahedron

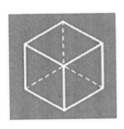 Earth - The Hexahedron

Transforming Your Home

You will need to understand the bagua map of your home if you are to decorate your home through Feng Shui to promote good chi. However, that doesn't mean that there aren't some tips and tricks that you should try to put in each and every room. Before continuing you must create a bagua map of your house.

Find out how each room of your house is oriented, and remember to put activating elements into the room as shown below. There are still some basic tips for best colors and Feng Shui for your home, but you do need to personalize it to your home's layout.

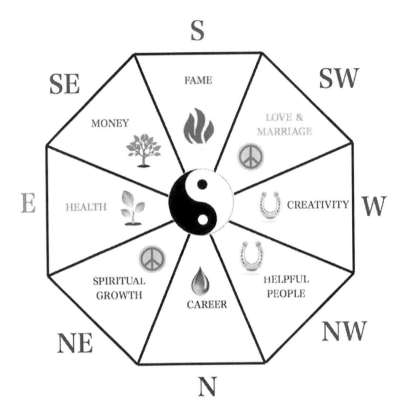

Photo Credit: (c) Rodika Tchi

Quick Guide by Directions

You may not have time for a bagua map just yet, but if you're looking for something a little more simple and comprehensive, then you'll find that this quick guide is for you. Decorate based on the bagua map above, and refer to the tips outlined below for more detail. Using a bagua map doesn't have to be hard, and when you apply it with this quick guide and the tips you'll find for each room, you'll be able to create a house that is, energy-wise, in perfect balance. Remember that the colors are all connected to certain elements and themes, as the bagua map explains.

East Rooms:

If you are looking for a room that is facing east, no matter the purpose of the room itself, you would need to incorporate the colors related of the wood element. These colors are generally green and brown. Blue and black can also be good colors for an east facing room, but you do need to limit your fire colors such as purple and red, in order to keep the energy in balance.

Southeast Rooms:

When decorating a southeast room, you'll want it to have the same colors as those near the east area. These colors are green, brown, blue and black.

However, you would want to add in golden tones as well, because this is considered to be the money area of your home (which you'll see in the bagua map diagram above). This is meant to help to bring wealth and prosperity energy into your home.

South Room Colors:

Southern oriented rooms are ruled by the element of fire. When you are trying to create a positive chi energy in any south facing room, you'll want to use fire and wood element colors. This includes yellow (but a strong yellow), green, brown, orange, red, pink and even purple. You will need to limit colors like black and blue in your south facing rooms, or it could disrupt the balance of chi.

Southwest Room Colors:

The southwest room is ruled by earth colors, and therefore you need them to be warm and nurturing colors. You can use the color of clay, earthenware, bricks, pottery, and fire colors are also good for the southwest room. When you do pick fire colors, go for coral, pink, or even red. It is connected to love and marriage, and there is a touch of romantic energy in this room, so you can add blush skin tones, floral prints or even sensual fabrics to decorate it.

West Room Colors:

You'll need to add a strong metal energy to this room, which means you need to use gray and white coloring, but limit your white. Make sure that metallic finishes are present, and nourishing earthy colors are good as well. There are colors you should avoid in your west room, and those are deep blues, blacks, and fiery colors.

Northwest Room Colors:

This is also a room that will love the element of metal, so greys and whites are going to help bring this room alive. You'll want limit het white but, use grays and metallic finishes. Remember to avoid fiery colors, blues, and limit your blacks. You'll want to have a Buddha statue or anything that helps you reach out spiritually in this room, because rooms oriented this way are connected to heavenly blessings.

North Room Colors:

Northern facing rooms are great with the water element, and so you can add water elements into the room. Blue and black are the proper colors for here, and you want to use some white, gray, and metallic finishes to add a metallic energy in the room as well. Make sure that you limit the presence of earth colors in this room.

Northeast Room Colors:

The elements that will need to be infused into the chi of this room is fire and earth. This is a room that is connected to spiritual growth and spiritual cultivation. You may want to add a golden Buddha that will express the energy that you want. Earthy colors are welcome in this room, but you can also use red, purple, magenta and different reds.

Living Room

You already know what to put in your living room as far as colors are concerned from the section above. However, there are some Feng Shui tips that are perfect for your living room. There are certain shapes that will help to generate a happy and peaceful Feng Shui in your living area. If your living room faces north, then you'll want wavy shapes that will resemble the flow of water. This will create a flowing energy in the room that allows for prosperity and change.

However, your furniture arrangement will be extremely important in decorating your living room for the best energy as well. You need to make sure that both your family members and guests feel at ease. When you look at your living room, remember that chi flows like water. Is there any place that you feel will box energy off? Are you directing energy to flow out a window or door before it can nourish your environment? Make sure that you have an open floor plan that allows for movement.

Tips:

1. You will need sunlight and ventilation because this room is meant to be uplifting. This will make sure that you have only positive chi.
2. Your living room needs to be comfortable to live in, or you will be inviting *sha chi* (negative energy).
3. You should be able to see the main door when you sit on the main sofa because it allows you to welcome chi into your life.
4. You can place a bowl of coins, crystals, or any other monetary object on the coffee table if it is in the money part of your house.

5. You will want to hang positive pictures and artwork on the walls so that you attract happiness.
6. You should always cover your TV when it is off or it will act as a mirror, which is bad Feng Shui.

To Avoid:

1. You should avoid putting your window behind the main sofa. This is because you are not receiving nature energy when you face away from the outside, and it can also block chi from coming into your home.
2. You should never have a mirror facing something negative such as dirt or clutter. This will attract negative energy into your home by reflecting it back into the room.
3. You should avoid hanging any pictures that reflect a negative emotion such a as war, loneliness, crime, or anyone that is sad or depressed.
4. Even if you have a northern facing living room, you need to you'll want to avoid any painting

that depicts a violent or turbulent sea. Never hang up a picture in your living room that depicts struggle, or you'll be inviting struggle into your own life.

Kitchen

Your kitchen is the part of your home that is essential to nourish and keep you sustained, and so you'll want to always have good energy in your kitchen. It is extremely important that you know what you can and can't place in your kitchen for the right energy. Food gives you energy, and you need to have a high healing quality of energy in the room that you cook it in.

In Feng Shui, it is believed that everything you put into the room and surround yourself with has an energy to it, so you will find that the food that you keep in your kitchen will have an effect on the energy of the room as well.

Tips:

1. Always surround yourself with good food that is healthy for you. If you can afford organic food, it is best to store it in the room openly to invite natural elements and health and prosperity into the kitchen.
2. Use aromatic herbs to increase the positive energy in your kitchen.
3. Fresh food is also important to have in your kitchen to promote positive chi.
4. You should try to keep about one to two feet between your kitchen sink and your stove. If

this is not an option because of the size of your kitchen, you'll want to put a small plant or aromatic herbs between the two to help keep the water and fire from opposing each other. In terms of energy, you should try to keep your fridge and your stove separated as well for the same reason.

5. Make sure that you don't allow leaking faucets or taps anywhere in your house. No less your kitchen. This will encourage the draining of fortune.
6. It is best if you can place your sink in the North East or North part of your kitchen.
7. Make sure that your kitchen is clean so that it does not affect the healthy energy.
8. Choose colors based on the placement of your kitchen, but if it is near the fire section of your home, then you'd want to use the color yellow, because it is good for digestion.

To Avoid:

1. Don't allow for anything that is rotting to stay in your kitchen because this is allowing the negative energy to fill a healthy space.
2. Do not allow your trash can to stay open, or it will cause the same effect.
3. You should avoid your kitchen being at the center or your home or near the front door. Your kitchen should also never be placed under a toilet on the second floor. It is best to keep it from being placed under a bedroom as well.
4. You'll want to clean your kitchen as often as possible, because if you have a soiled platform or utensil, bad chi can accumulate in the area.
5. You should never place your stove directly in front of the entrance to your kitchen.
6. Try to avoid placing your stove where you will face south to cook, or it is believed that your family could face monetary losses.
7. Try to avoid placing a kitchen's entrance in a corner or this can cause a blockage of chi.

Bathroom

A bathroom can be located at any part of your home, and this means that it can be anywhere on the bagua map of your home. It could be located in the area for luck, wealth, love or anything else. A bathroom is known to drain away good luck and fortune from whatever area it is located in. Logically, a bathroom will have a strong correlation with the element of water. Keep this in mind when choosing colors and materials for your bathroom design. Try to use as much natural materials as possible for a peaceful, calm bathing environment.

Tips:

1. You should always keep the bathroom door closed, so that the energy does not escape into the rest of the house. If you do keep your bathroom door open, it will affect the chi of other rooms.
2. Make sure that your toilet lid is closed for a similar reason.
3. Your bathroom should receive sunlight and fresh air as often as possible to clear out any remaining negative energy.
4. Make sure that you keep the windows, ventilators, and doors to your bathroom clean so that negative chi does not accumulate.
5. If any of your curtains are stained or torn, replace them with new ones.
6. It is wise to place a mirror on the door of the bathroom so that the chi to bounce back into the house. It will keep it from entering your bathroom at all.
7. It increases the positive chi in the bathroom if you have air freshener or aromatic oils for when you take a long bath or shower.

To Avoid:

1. As always, avoid clutter in your bathroom. Your bathroom is already too small, and clutter will only increase the already high chances of bad energy.
2. Old and worn out things need to be taken out of your bathroom and never left there, and this does include tooth brushes and towels.
3. You should try and avoid your bathroom being located at the center of your home, facing a bedroom, dining room or kitchen.
4. Make sure that nothing leaks in your bathroom. This is something that needs to be checked regularly because of the amount of plumbing in this room. Leaking pipes means monetary loss.
5. If you want metallic wind chimes, never place them in the North West, west, or north corner of your bathroom.
6. It is normal to have a mirror in your bathroom, but you should try and avoid the mirrors directly reflecting the toilet seats.

Bedroom

A bedroom provides two purposes. It provides you with a place to be comfortable and relaxed so that you can sleep, which is important for managing tasks and responsibilities during the day. The second purpose of the bedroom is to give a romantic privacy for sensual pleasure. The bedroom, because of its two major purposes, can be divided into these two sections. Make sure your room design is both sensual and calming. Use a natural look with soft colors where possible.

Tips for the First Purpose (Relaxation):

1. You should try to promote a comfortable and open floor plan with our bedroom, to make sure that it is inviting and comfortable. A bigger bedroom will work best.
2. Usually wooden beds are best in a bedroom, but make sure that they are a high quality wood. Pressed wood will not provide the grounding element that you need.
3. The bed's headboard should always be placed against a wall.
4. It promotes the best energy and flow of chi when the bed is facing in a way that you can see the entrance to your bedroom.
5. Equality is great to have in your bedroom, so putting identical lamps on either side of your bed is best to promote equality in your relationship.
6. It is best to keep the energy in the bedroom fresh, so you need to make sure to open windows and doors regularly so that it can get a proper flow of chi. it is also important that it has proper sunlight.

7. Promote happiness and joy by hanging pictures that are about joy, happiness, and good memories.
8. Try to select natural and luxurious linen for bed sheets, pillow covers, and quit sets. This promotes a sensual energy flow to your room.

To Avoid for the First Purpose (Relaxation):

1. Make sure that the placement of the bed is not in front of the bathroom door.
2. It is important that you do not have an AC vent behind the bed directly, or it will block the flow of chi.
3. It is bad fortune to have a mirror reflect your body when you're lying in bed. If you don't have a choice, then cover the mirror before you go to bed.
4. Anything heavy or large should not hang above the bed.
5. You should keep TV, PCs, laptops and other electronic devices outside of the bedroom because it blocks the natural energy of the room, making it less relaxing.

6. You need to avoid work related objects in your room such as a desk, exercise gear or anything else. You should also never discuss work in the bedroom because this will give the room a negative chi.

Tips for the Second Purpose (Sensuality):

1. You need to freshen up the room in your air using an air freshener or a purifier.
2. If you dress in sensual colors when you're in the room, it will help to promote a romantic chi. having these clothes will also help to make sure that the room has a romantic energy to it.
3. Hanging romantic photos of yourself or just general pictures and paintings will help as well.
4. Skin tone colors as well as light red, chocolate brown, and even pink will help to make sure that you have a romantic chi flowing within the bedroom.

To Avoid for the Second Purpose (Sensuality):

1. You should try to keep family members and friends, including pictures, out of your bedroom so that it doesn't decrease the romantic feel of the room.
2. You should never keep things that remind you of your ex in this room or it will cause sha chi (negative energy).
3. Make sure that you avoid blue and black in your bedroom as much as possible because it will kill your sexual drive.
4. You need to avoid hanging religious pictures when you can as well because it will also decrease an intimate chi in the room.
5. Avoiding bright lights is best, because it can be too harsh for a romantic feel. Dimmed lights are more sensual.

Children's Room

A child's room is a personal place that makes them feel safe. This is why it should always be personalized, no matter what area it falls in on the bagua map. You should still stay mindful of using the colors that are best for the use of the room and the person it belongs to. Of course, you'll need to keep the clutter down to a minimum as well, which is sometimes rather difficult when you have a child. Children are sometimes unmotivated to clean up after themselves, but making sure that they have organizational tools will help a lot with this.

Tips:

1. Start by making sure that the room has many organizational tools to help make sure there are no issues with clutter or negative chi.
2. Make sure that the curtains are lightweight and easy to move, to let natural light into the room.
3. Keep plants in the room to help with natural energy in the room, as children do not connect with nature enough. It provides grounding. They will also help to purify the room of negative plants.
4. Allow your child to help plan the room's design as well. Even if you guide them through the planning process, it'll help to make sure that their personal energy and creativity is in the room.

To Avoid:

1. Make sure that they have only happy pictures in the room. There should be no sad pictures, dolls, clowns or other sad toys present in the child's bedroom.

2. Make sure that you get all of the old and torn out blankets, pillow cases, or toys out of the room.
3. Avoid whites, as it will make the energy too masculine and cold. Greys and metallic colors are to be avoided if possible as well. Unless the room falls in that area of the bagua map, and then you'll want bright colors that have a metallic finish.

Office

Your home office needs to be clean and crisp without being empty. Make sure that you decorate it in the colors that it falls into, but you also need to keep clutter out of the office. Keep a trash can that is closed to start, and make sure that your furniture is as new as possible. Anything old or falling apart is allowing negative energy in your space.

Tips:

1. Make sure that you sit in the farthest corner form the entrance to your office. This will give you a commanding position of the room, allowing you to control your office space and promote a controlled energy.
2. Make sure to keep your chair where your back will be towards a wall or a corner for support. This will make sure that your energy goes out into the room.

3. If you have control over the placement of your office, having a tree outside the window and behind you is supposed to give you a significant natural support.
4. Pick either the east, north, or southeast and place an aquarium or tabletop fountain. Black and blue are great colors for an office, as they allow for a flowing chi and healthy energy, which promotes creativity.
5. Make sure to balance yin and yang when you decorate your workspace. Make sure that light and dark are balanced in furniture, flooring, and colors.

Tips to Avoid:

1. Make sure that you don't place mirrors in your office, as they can reflect any negative energy from frustration.
2. Don't arrange your office in such a way that it looks into the corridor, stairs, closet or any other closed, small space that will trap the flow of chi.

3. Don't allow yourself to face away from the door or look into a window. This will direct your chi out of your space or allow it to accumulate negatively.
4. Do not directly sit in front of the door because you will be in the path of negative energy.

Garden

Once again, you'll need a bagua guide for your garden. You want to map out your garden just like you would map out your home. A Feng Shui garden has a 'mountain', greenery and a water element. This is why you'll that many Feng Shui gardens feature a water element. For a mountain aspect, anything that is raised will work. This can be raised flower beds, or you can go with decorative rocks. A real life 'mountain' or hill is not required.

Tips:

1. Do add a water element. This can be a fountain, a bird bath, or even a koi pond. You cannot skip the water element in your Feng Shui garden!
2. You will need a fire element. This can be lighting, a fire pit, or even lanterns.
3. Arbors, planters, and wind chimes are also important when you are looking for a metal element in your garden.
4. Abor, planting boxes, or benches will show the wood element, but trees can help as well.

5. Earth will need to be added as well, and this can be done as clay planters, wooden planters, and the right type of soil.

To Avoid:

1. Do not place the water and fire next to each other without something in between them. Plants will be necessary.
2. Do not assume that the earth element doesn't need represented. If you do not give it proper representation, you are not balancing yin and yang. You will attract sha chi (negative energy). The earth element will come naturally with a large area for plants.
3. Avoid too many unnatural colors in your garden such as neon's, yellows, or bright pinks.

Declutter & Simplify

You already know that Feng Shui is meant to bring good vibrations to your home and clear it of *sha chi* (negative energy). However, that's not going to work if you keep broken, soiled, or even damaged items around your home. You need to regularly take out the old, embracing the new. This will lso renew the chi inside your living space: keep your living space clean and free of unnecessary items. A fresh spring cleaning is very refreshing to your homes chi. But a bug declutter session really can be done in any season. Negative energy will disrupt the flow of chi throughout your space, and so each room needs to be clutter free whenever possible. Let's look at some strategies to start decluttering your home.

Strategy to Declutter

The first thing that you need to know when you start to declutter any home for any reason, is that you'll need to go about doing this room by room. You can't expect to declutter your *entire* house in a day, and you certainly can't expect to do every room at once. Pick a room to start with, and then take a trash bag in the room. Stepwise decluttering is often the most effective way of going about it. You will need to throw some things away, and deciding what to throw away doesn't have to be hard at all. Here are three steps to consider when decluttering.

Step 1: Take Out the Old

You don't have to throw away something that is old simply because it's old. You may have old furniture that is still good, for example. These items should stay. However, if the furniture is torn, you'll want to recover it. If it's broken, you'll want to get rid of it.

Remember that in Feng Shui, you basically are what you see. You cannot be around broken and torn items. This will disrupt the positive flow of energy in the room. So throw out everything you don't need as well. Have you really ever used that decorative candy jar? If it's not useful, then you don't need it. There are decorative pieces that can stay, but you don't want to start collecting decorative pieces that make the space feel too crowded.

Step 2: Clear Your Surfaces

So you may need everything that is left in the room after you've already taken out the old and broken, but that doesn't mean you need your surfaces to be clear. You'll need to work on one surface at a time. Take the coffee table for an example. You don't need books on your coffee table. You don't even need coasters always sitting on your coffee table. These should have places of their own. If you need the books in the living room, don't just stack them. Find a home for everything: add shelves and organization.

You can buy organizational tools already made with different boxes, decorative containers, and shelves, or you can use a DIY project. If you have a coffee table that has space underneath it, then utilize that space. Don't just keep everything out on the top and in the open. You'll find one great way to add a wood element to your room and shelves above. It's a DIY project where you turn a ladder into a shelving unit by inserting boards. If you're trying to add a metal element, you could always paint it a metallic color or with a metallic finish.

Step 3: Rearrange for Simplicity

After the declutter process, it's time for simplification. You've gotten rid of what's broken, what you don't need, and found everything a home. However, you need to rearrange to make sure that you have everything grouped together properly. One of the main reasons that spaces get cluttered in the first place, is because you don't want to take the effort to put things away. If you're looking for coasters, you don't want to go to the other side of the room to get them, and you certainly don't want to always walk to put them back up.

You may try to argue with yourself, saying you aren't that lazy, but most people are. You want everything to be easily accessible, and that means you'll want to store the coasters on a side table nearby or under the coffee table itself. It really can be that easy. Just take each surface and what you need, and try to make sure that everything is arranged in a way that allows for the flow of positive energy while still providing easy accessibility.

Positive Energy Essentials

When you're decluttering your house, it's just like rearranging it. That means it will disrupt the chi of your household. Feng Shui is meant to promote positive chi and a positive flow of energy, so you don't want the decluttering process to interrupt this either. The first thing to remember is to never let yourself to become frustrated. You also need to make sure that just because you are finding a home for something, you're keeping the bagua map in mind.

For example, you may not like the fountain where it's sitting and can find a new place for it, but you never want to put a water element in the south corner of the room. As long as you are staying calm through the process, referencing your bagua map, and not keeping broken or torn items around, this should not create a negative energy.

Becoming Zen:

Perfect Feng Shui Home Tips

You now know every essential principle in order to improve the Feng Shui energy flow in your living space. However, there are still some tips and tricks that you can employ in your home to make sure that you create and maintain a Zen atmosphere.

There's more to Feng Shui than just the bagua map, despite it being the building block to direct you with your home arrangement. Positive energy is essential to maintaining and attracting a positive lifestyle and fortune. To avoid misfortune, you need a healthy and happy atmosphere surrounding you, and these tips should help.

Tip #1 Aromatherapy Always

Chances are that if your house smells bad, then you are attracting negative energy. If your house doesn't have any smell, you aren't attracting anything. Good or bad. If you have a positive scent lingering in your home, then you are promoting positive energy and positive fortune. That's why you should always use aromatherapy. There are many easy and effective solutions, such as burning essential oils, or if you would rather something even simpler than that, you can use an oil diffuser that you refill about every week. Air fresheners are great to keep around as well.

Tip #2 Keep Garbage Covered

You don't want garbage just sitting around. Instead, always keep the garbage covered. When you're buying trash cans, get trash cans that have a lid on them. If you're cleaning up, don't leave the bag just sitting there. When you take a break, it's fine to leave it there temporarily. It is not okay to leave it there overnight. If you do have a waste bin that doesn't have a lid, clear it out every night so that the negative energy does not linger in the room, especially the kitchen space.

Tip #3 Quality Air & Light Matters

Aromatherapy helps, but you'll find that it's not quality air and light in your home improves the general energy of the house. It can be as easy as leaving your window or door open. Remembering to pull back curtains to let natural light into a room is also important, because it helps to clear out the impurities in the energy of the room. Try to only use airflow and light from a natural source.

Tip #4 Plants in Every Room

Every room can have a plant in your house, and it doesn't all have to be something easy like a fern. There are many different types of plants you can use from a cactus, to air plants, to flowers in a vase or pot, to even something as simple as that bamboo or a bonsai tree. Base the type of plant you're placing in the room to the type of room that you have.

If you are working in an office, you may want something that adds greenery to the crisp, clean room. Something large like a fern will help. If it is the bedroom, then you'll want something that gives a romantic feel. Prim roses on the windowsill or any flowers on the nightstand can usually help. Always make sure that you place it in the corner of the room, in order to represent the earth element.

Tip #5 Don't Overdo It

This is far too easy to do. And the committed Feng Shui adopter will certainly find themselves in a situation where they try to overdo it. But honestly, simple is better when it comes to Feng Shui. There may be lucky numbers, colors, or stones that you want to incorporate, and you can incorporate them into your house without incorporating them in every single room.

Make sure that each room has a simple approach to it and isn't too cluttered. Get rid of unwanted items, but no need to be overly minimalistic in your life. Decoration also has a purpose, and decorative items certainly should have a place in your home. If you do have a lot to go in one room, organization is going to be your best friend.

Get Started Today

Feng Shui doesn't have to wait. You can get started, and you don't have to buy anything expensive to do it. Use what you already have in your house. Add as you need to. You don't need to go out and buy a plant for every room right away. You can just get it as you go and when you can afford it. Sustainable change and spiritual change go hand in hand.

You don't need to get rid of all broken furniture at once. Get rid of it as you can replace it. You may not be able to do a total makeover to your house to make it positive right away, but getting rid of as much negativity as you can when you can will make a difference. Each small step that you take will lead you a little closer to having a home that is designed to promote a healthy, happy, and fortunate life.

Parting Words

Incorporating the art of Feng Shui into your daily life is a process. A tool to get closer to yourself. It is about the energy and balance within ourselves and our personal surroundings. Deep down inside, we already know everything about our inner being and inner life energy, but that knowledge is found only in our subconscious mind. Feng Shui will never be fast or miracle cure, but it will certainly be a helpful *tool* in the process of getting to know both yourself and your personal inner energy.

I hope this short guidebook has given you some more in-depth insight into the topic of Feng Shui and will lead you on a path towards a better and happier life. One that will not be without darkness, but one that you enable yourself to *deal* with any personal imbalances or problems in a much better way. If you liked anything you read in this book, or if you simply want to help me in my writing journey, it would be much appreciated if you could leave a review for this book. By writing an honest review, your opinion will help other people to make a decision about getting a book like this to help them in their personal spiritual journey.

My eternal gratitude to you, as a reader, for reading this book. Taking the time to learn about spiritual concepts is valuable and potentially life-changing. Therefore I as a writer am grateful for every soul I might have touched in my writing journey. Hopefully you are now a little bit more knowledgeable on the topic and will be able to start focusing on balancing your inner energy. A journey into the spiritual world is always an interesting opportunity to discover more about life, and discover more about who you are as a person. All the best in your life, and my gratitude for giving me the opportunity to bring you closer to yourself.

Antonio Barros

Spirituality and Psychology Expert

Made in the USA
Lexington, KY
26 July 2016